LADYBIRD HISTORIES

First World War

History consultant: Terry Charman, Imperial War Museum
Map illustrator: Martin Sanders

A catalogue record for this book is available from the British Library

Published by Ladybird Books Ltd
80 Strand, London, WC2R 0RL
A Penguin Company

001

ISBN: 978-0-72327-085-0
Printed in China

PICTURE CREDITS
The publisher would like to thank the following for their kind permission to
reproduce their photographs:
44tl © Corbis; 44tr © Swim Ink 2, LLC/Corbis

LADYBIRD HISTORIES

First World War

Written by Brian Williams
Main illustrations by Nick Hardcastle
Cartoon illustrations by Clive Goodyer

Contents

Introduction

The First World War started in 1914 and lasted for four years. It was a war fought mainly in Europe, with battles on land, at sea and in the air. There was fighting in the Middle East and in parts of Africa, too. Because so many of the largest, richest and strongest nations in the world took part, people at the time called it the Great War. Today it is known as the First World War.

A lasting impact

The war changed the world. In Europe, old empires, such as Austria-Hungary and the Ottoman (Turkish) Empire that had once ruled many other countries, collapsed and new nations emerged.

One First World War soldier, Harry Patch, who joined the British Army in 1916, remembered a friend, *'I held his hand for the last thirty seconds of his life.'* When he visited the graves of comrades who died in the war he said, *'Any one of them could have been me.'* Harry was one of the longest-lived survivors of the First World War. He died in 2009, aged 111 years.

Never forget

Fighting ended at 11 o'clock on 11 November 1918. This was the 11th hour of the 11th month. Every year on Remembrance Sunday we remember the people who have died in all wars.

During the war, poppies grew on the battlefields of Europe. People then began to wear paper poppies in memory of those who had lost their lives. This tradition is still carried on today.

The World in 1914

In 1914, Europe consisted of large empires and many smaller nations. With its great cities, factories, roads and railways, Europe was rich, but it was also divided. Britain, France and Germany wanted to expand their trade and influence around the world, and rule large overseas empires.

Arms race

In the years running up to the war, Germany, Britain and France competed to have the most powerful navy. Military and economic tensions were running high between European nations in 1914, so only a spark was needed to set off a war.

Each country wanted bigger and better ships and guns for their armies.

European tensions

With Europe divided, countries began to take sides. Germany and Austria-Hungary were on one side, with France and Russia on the other. Britain joined France and Russia to form the Allies, while Japan was also allied to Britain. Germany, Austria-Hungary and the Ottoman Empire became the Central Powers. Italy began the war as a neutral country, before joining the Allies in May 1915.

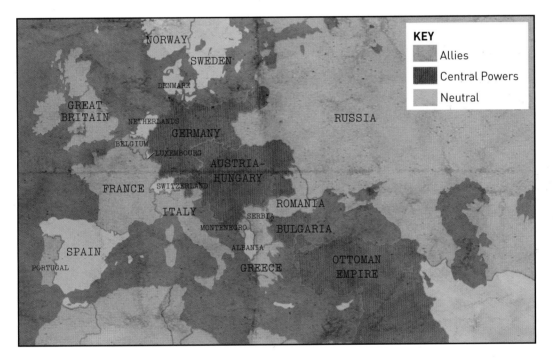

The rest of the world

Europe's largest countries had huge empires around the world, with many colonies under their control. These colonies became involved in Europe's rising tensions, too. However, across the Atlantic Ocean, the fast-growing United States of America (USA) took little interest in Europe's quarrels.

The First Shot

On 28 June 1914, a Bosnian-Serb named Gavrilo Princip shot and assassinated the heir to the Austro-Hungarian throne, Archduke Franz Ferdinand, in Sarajevo, Bosnia. Austria-Hungary blamed Serbia for the murder and on 28 July 1914 declared war against them. Serbia asked Russia for help, and Germany had previously promised to support Austria-Hungary against Russia. Britain and France were Russia's allies so they backed Russia, even if this meant war.

The shot that killed Archduke Franz Ferdinand sparked the 'war to end all wars'.

Preparing for war

On 1 August 1914, Germany went to war with Russia, and just two days later it declared war on France. Germany's plan was to knock France out of the war, before moving on to attack Russia. German armies marched into neutral Belgium on 4 August, with the aim of reaching France. Britain promised to help Belgium and so went to war with Germany, as did France and Russia. The First World War had begun.

Huge armies got ready for war, with millions of soldiers on the move across Europe. They travelled by train or tramped along roads with wagons and horses. Army soldiers checked guns and defences, while generals made battle plans. Large guns, known as artillery, were pulled into position and battleships headed out to sea.

Kitted out

British soldiers carried a personal kit that included a razor, soap, spare socks and perhaps a family photo, as well as a spade, hand grenades, ammunition and a rifle.

British soldiers wore khaki uniforms.

The German uniform was grey.

The French wore red and blue in 1914.

Britain Goes to War

The British people believed France's big army would quickly beat the Germans, so only a small British army, the British Expeditionary Force, was sent to France to help.

Later in the war, people sang popular songs as the men departed such as: 'Are We Downhearted? No!'; 'Good-bye-ee'; 'Pack Up Your Troubles in Your Old Kit-bag and Smile, Smile, Smile' and 'Take Me Back to Dear Old Blighty [Britain]'.

Like most soldiers, Captain Douglas H. Bell was eager to fight. He wrote in his diary on 7 November 1914, '*I think we all treat it [the war] as a bit of a game...*'

Many men happily went to war, believing they would be home by Christmas.

The British Empire

For most people in Britain, the British Empire was more important than Europe. Britain's empire was the biggest, and it ruled more than 400 million people around the world. On school maps, the countries of the British Empire were coloured red. Children were taught that Britain was the 'mother country' of this vast empire-family. Many children had relatives who lived in Canada, Australia or South Africa, and others knew people living in India or Africa. Every year on 24 May, Queen Victoria's birthday, children dressed up to celebrate Empire Day. They waved flags and sang patriotic songs. The British Army included large numbers of soldiers from colonies across the empire. Many of these troops had never left their home countries before.

Families at war

Britain's King George V and the German emperor, Kaiser Wilhelm II, were cousins (both were grandsons of Queen Victoria). To complicate matters further, Tsar Nicholas II of Russia was married to Queen Victoria's grandaughter Alexandra.

King George V   Kaiser Wilhelm II   Tsar Nicholas II

A Soldier's Duties

At the start of the war the British Army had about 250,000 soldiers ready to fight. Many former soldiers were in the reserves – a group of men who had finished their service in the Army but who were ready to rejoin. There were more part-time soldiers in the Territorial Army for home defence, making over 700,000 troops in total. Lord Kitchener, a soldier known as the 'Empire's Hero', called for even more volunteers. More than 2 million men joined Kitchener's 'New Armies'. Many of them would not return home.

Signing up

At the outbreak of war men formed queues at recruiting offices. They all wanted to sign up and fight for their country. It was thought men would be more willing to join up if they could serve with people they already knew. Battalions of men from the same local area, or who worked in the same industry, became known as the 'Pals' battalions. In August 1914, Lord Derby tried to raise the first battalion in Liverpool. Within days, Liverpool had enlisted enough men to form four Pals battalions.

Training and preparation

Every new British recruit had to undergo a medical test to make sure he was fit to fight. Some men failed because of poor eyesight or general ill health. Once a soldier had passed the test, he took an oath of loyalty to the king and became a member of the British Army. Training was tough and new soldiers quickly learned to obey orders.

Soldiers were taught to fire a rifle and fight with a bayonet. The gunners learned to work in teams to fire big guns.

Cavalry soldiers rode horses. The British Army began the war with 25,000 horses, but soon had 500,000 from farms and stables, and from abroad.

The men shared barracks and tents with other soldiers. There, they would eat their meals and clean their kits together.

Soldiers needed to be disciplined and fit so they practised drill every day. This involved marching and following other instructions very strictly.

The Western Front

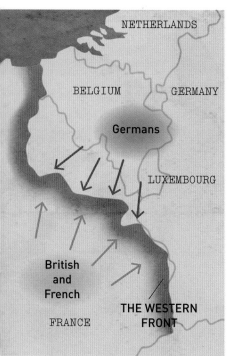

The German plan was to capture Paris, the capital of France, and win a quick victory. But the Germans were stopped by British and French soldiers in a battle at the River Marne in September 1914. With each side able to stop the other's attack, neither could make progress.

The attacks failed because this was a new kind of war with weapons more powerful than had been used before. A single machine gun could shoot down hundreds of marching soldiers and quick-firing artillery was able to flatten woods, blast down walls and destroy entire villages.

German guns fired a type of shell that travelled faster than the speed of sound. British soldiers called it the 'whizzbang' because they heard the 'whizz' overhead before the 'bang' of the gun.

The landscape

The two armies stayed put, facing one another along the Western Front. This was a long winding line across western Europe (see map, opposite). Generals studied maps, wondering how and where to attack. Meanwhile the big guns on each side kept firing, bombarding the soldiers sheltering in holes in the ground. The holes got deeper and longer, becoming a network of trenches across France. With shells whistling overhead and bursting all around, the soldiers realized it was going to be a long war.

The Christmas truce

On Christmas Eve 1914, soldiers on both sides of the Western Front sang carols. The following day many troops observed an unofficial truce. Fighting stopped and religious services were held. Hundreds of British and German soldiers left the trenches and crossed no man's land (the area between the armies' trenches) to share chocolate, drinks and cigarettes. At the Front, a football match even took place between some British and German soldiers. Germany won the game 3-2.

Trench Warfare

The new weapons of the First World War meant that unprotected fighting in the open was impossible. The only way to survive was to dig trenches in which to live and fight. On the Western Front, millions of soldiers were stuck in these trenches.

Trench life alternated between periods of short, intense fighting and longer periods of boredom. Most enemy attacks took place at dawn and dusk, so all troops were ready at those times. During the day, men slept, wrote letters home or kept diaries.

Most soldiers spent ten days each month in the trenches, then 'came out of the line' for a rest. They marched to the nearest town or army camp for a hot bath and a meal, before returning to the trenches.

Wounded soldiers were treated at casualty stations by army doctors and nurses. Those who were badly wounded faced a long and uncomfortable journey to the field hospital. If they recovered from their injuries, the soldiers would return to the trenches.

Life in the trenches

Trench life was cold, wet and muddy. In some places on the Front, men, horses and guns got stuck, and wounded soldiers could even drown in the thick mud. Clothes and boots were permanently soaked and many soldiers got a painful condition called trench foot. Soldiers ate and slept in the trenches, or in cramped shelters called dugouts. Toilets were deep pits with wooden seats behind the main trench. The soldiers tried to keep the trenches clean, but rats were often seen scurrying about. When the guns paused, hot food was brought up but soldiers often lived on tinned beef, biscuits, bread and jam, and tea for days at a time.

An attack was called 'going over the top'. Officers blew whistles to signal for soldiers to leave their trenches. They walked or ran forward towards the enemy.

No Man's Land

To attack the enemy trenches, the soldiers had to cross no man's land. Both sides took every opportunity to attack the enemy, so any soldier popping his head up from cover, or leaving the trenches to rescue a wounded comrade, was considered a fair target.

One machine gun, firing up to 500 bullets a minute, could kill hundreds of soldiers during an attack. The near-constant firing of artillery turned fields and woods into wastelands, pitted with shell-holes. Some holes flooded with water so deep that the soldiers who fell in them drowned.

After men went 'over the top', they had to cut through tangled barbed wire and struggle through mud, with artillery shells exploding around them, hurling metal and dirt in all directions.

Grenades and gas

If attacking soldiers made it across no man's land and reached the enemy trenches, they would throw in hand grenades. These were small bombs that exploded about four seconds after being thrown. Poison gas was also used as a weapon. It was released from cans, or fired in shells. It drifted across the battlefield, killing or causing skin wounds, blindness and sickness. Soldiers put on gas masks when the 'Gas!' warning came. More than 90,000 soldiers from all nations were killed by poison gas.

Gas attack

On 22 April 1915 French-Algerian troops near the town of Ypres, Belgium, noticed a greenish cloud moving across no man's land towards them. This was the first time the German army successfully used deadly poison gas to attack its enemies. The gas attack wounded and killed many Allied soliders.

The Battle of the Somme

General
Douglas Haig

Marshal
Joseph Joffre

On 1 July 1916, a long and deadly battle between French and British armies on one side and the German army on the other began along the River Somme in France. Britain's General Douglas Haig and Marshal Joseph Joffre of France hoped their armies would break through the German trenches. The battle began with a week of gunfire that was supposed to smash gaps in the German defences and kill most of the German soldiers.

A long battle

But the plan failed – German soldiers took cover in deep bunkers and were largely unharmed. The German army fought back and on the first day of their counterattack, some 19,000 British soldiers were killed and 40,000 wounded. The fighting then continued throughout the summer of 1916.

Tank tactics

In September 1916, a new British invention rumbled into action – tanks. These were big, armoured vehicles with guns. The British hoped that the tanks would help them win, but the Battle of the Somme dragged on until November 1916. By then more than 1 million soldiers from across the British Empire, France and Germany had been killed or wounded. The British and French had gained only 8 miles of ground.

The name 'tank' (meaning water-carrier) disguised the fact that these were armoured fighting vehicles. The name stuck and is still used today.

Shell-shock and shootings

After months of battle, some soldiers became ill with shell-shock – a reaction to the horror of battle that is today called combat stress. These men could no longer fight. Some were accused of being cowards. Soldiers who refused to fight or deserted were put on trial by army courts. A small number of British soldiers found guilty of disobeying orders were shot by army firing squads.

The World at War

The fighting continued and became more intense on the Western Front. At the same time, the war was being fought in other parts of the world. Disagreements quickly turned into conflicts across Europe, the Middle East and Africa.

Germany and Austria-Hungary reached here

GERMANY

RUSSIA

Eastern Front

Russia reached here

AUSTRIA-HUNGARY

The Eastern Front

Germany and Austria-Hungary fought against Russia along the Eastern Front, which stretched across central and eastern Europe. Both sides fought huge battles in which they suffered heavy losses. The Russians, exhausted and poorly equipped, suffered the most, but were still fighting at the end of 1916.

War in Africa

Britain and Germany both had colonies in central, southern and eastern Africa. Fighting began when the German colonies were invaded by French, British and South African forces. In east Africa, a small German-led army of 5,000 men evaded 130,000 Allied troops until after the war in Europe ended in 1918.

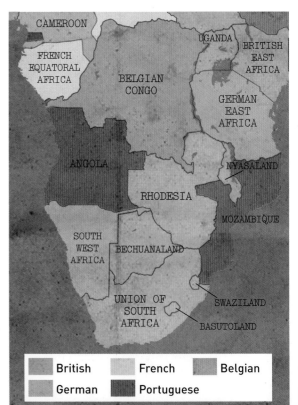

CAMEROON

UGANDA

BRITISH EAST AFRICA

FRENCH EQUATORAL AFRICA

BELGIAN CONGO

GERMAN EAST AFRICA

ANGOLA

NYASALAND

RHODESIA

MOZAMBIQUE

SOUTH WEST AFRICA

BECHUANALAND

UNION OF SOUTH AFRICA

SWAZILAND

BASUTOLAND

British   French   Belgian
German   Portuguese

The Middle East

In October 1914, the Ottoman Empire, which ruled much of the Middle East, sided with Germany and declared a jihad (holy war) against Russia, France and Britain. Germany hoped that Ottoman involvement would weaken Russia and also damage Britain's trade routes to India and the Far East through the Suez Canal.

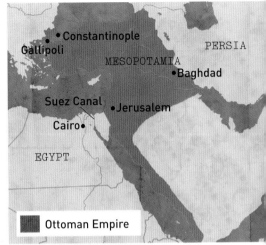

A supply of oil from the Middle East was essential to fuel Britain's military and industrial war effort. An alliance between Germany and the Ottoman Empire threatened the supply, so in 1914 British and Indian troops invaded Mesopotamia (modern Iraq) to secure the pipeline. After three years of fighting, they captured Baghdad in March 1917.

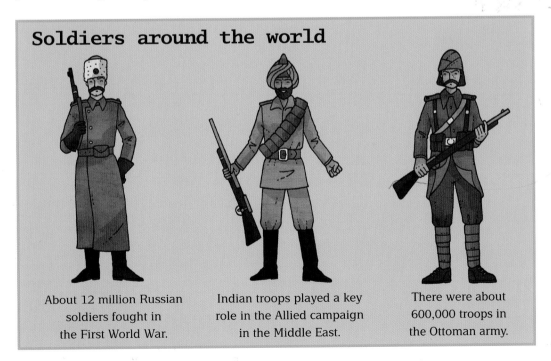

Soldiers around the world

About 12 million Russian soldiers fought in the First World War.

Indian troops played a key role in the Allied campaign in the Middle East.

There were about 600,000 troops in the Ottoman army.

Gallipoli

In early 1915, Britain and France wanted to help their ally Russia by capturing the Ottoman capital of Constantinople (present-day Istanbul) and forcing the Ottoman Empire out of the war. They tried to send ships through the Dardanelles – the strip of sea that separates European Turkey from the larger Asian part of the country. But the plan failed. The Ottoman army had put mines in the sea and had guns on land, so it was able to easily and successfully attack the Allied ships.

A new plan

A second attack was planned. Soldiers from Britain, India, Australia and New Zealand, as well as French troops, would land at Gallipoli in Turkey. On 25 April 1915, British, Australian and New Zealand soldiers landed safely, while French soldiers staged a distraction in the south.

However, Ottoman soldiers were waiting in the hills above the beaches. The Allies thought Gallipoli would be lightly defended, but Germany had equipped the Ottoman army with modern rifles and machine guns. There was chaos and confusion among the Allied soldiers, and though they fought bravely for many months, they had to withdraw at the end of 1915. More than 40,000 Allied soldiers and 60,000 Ottoman soldiers died.

Australian and New Zealand soldiers were called 'ANZACs' (Australia and New Zealand Army Corps). 25 April is Anzac Day in Australia and New Zealand, when people honour the men who fought at Gallipoli and all wars.

One man and his donkey

Australian soldier John Simpson Kirkpatrick rescued wounded men at Gallipoli with the help of a donkey he named Duffy. Together they carried wounded soldiers to the beach. Simpson was shot and killed on 19 May 1915, but Duffy was rescued when the Allies left Gallipoli.

Desert War

One of the major campaigns of the war took place in the deserts of the Middle East. British and Indian soldiers joined forces with Arab leaders in a revolt against Ottoman rule in the area. Soldiers rode horses and camels across the deserts of Palestine and Arabia to attack railways and towns. One British hero of this desert war was the army officer T. E. Lawrence, later known as Lawrence of Arabia.

Lawrence of Arabia

Lawrence studied history at Oxford University, England. He first went to the Middle East in 1909 and learned to speak Arabic. After working as an intelligence officer in Cairo, Egypt, in 1916, he was sent by the British Army to encourage the Arab leaders to oppose their Ottoman rulers. He led a number of raids and attacks on Ottoman targets, and campaigned on behalf of the Arabs.

T. E. Lawrence is remembered as a legendary figure of the First World War. He told his story in his book, *Seven Pillars of Wisdom*.

Jerusalem

The Arab Revolt against the Ottoman Empire began in June 1916. British troops joined the Arab soldiers to drive out the Turks and capture key places in early 1917. Later that year, the British Army invaded Palestine and General Allenby led his army into Jerusalem on 11 December.

The following year, British troops pushed north towards Damascus in Syria, while Lawrence's Arab army fought in the Palestinian desert. With the capture of Damascus in 1918 the desert war was over and so, too, was Ottoman rule of the Arabs.

Jerusalem is a holy city for Christians, Jews and Muslims. When the British Army entered the city in 1917, General Allenby got down from his horse and walked as a mark of respect.

War at Sea

In 1914, Britain had the world's strongest navy, with forty-two battleships, battle-cruisers and many smaller ships, including cruisers and destroyers. The Royal Navy's job was to defend Britain, hunt and destroy enemy ships, and keep the seas safe for British trade. This meant protecting ships carrying supplies to Britain and stopping supplies reaching Germany.

The Grand Fleet of battleships was based in Britain, but smaller fleets regularly crossed the world's oceans. Germany had fewer battleships, but sent fast lone raiders to sink British cargo ships. The German warship *Emden* sank fifteen ships before it, in turn, was sunk in November 1914 during a battle with the Australian warship *Sydney* in the Pacific Ocean.

The Battle of Jutland

The only major sea battle of the First World War was between the British and Germans in May 1916. This was the Battle of Jutland. It took place in the North Sea, with more than 250 British and German ships involved. Battleships blindly fired at vessels through smoke and mist, and at times neither fleet knew where the other was. There was no clear winner. The British Royal Navy lost fourteen ships and Germany lost eleven. The German fleet did not return for a second battle, which left the British free to 'rule the waves' and cut off Germany's trade by sea.

Brave boy sailor

Jack Cornwell was only sixteen when he fought at the Battle of Jutland. He was a member of the gun crew aboard HMS Chester. While others lay dead or injured, Cornwell stayed on watch despite being badly wounded. He died of his injuries in hospital later and was awarded the Victoria Cross for bravery — one of the youngest ever VC winners.

Floating bombs, called mines, were laid to blow up and sink enemy ships. Areas of sea with lots of mines were called minefields.

Submarine War

The war at sea was also fought below the waves, and much of the Battle of Jutland actually took place under the water. Submarines were still a new invention but could easily sink a battleship with torpedoes. Although submarines spent a lot of time at the surface, they were very hard to find. When a submarine captain saw an enemy ship through the periscope, the gun was fired to sink the vessel.

U-boats

The German word for submarine is Unterseeboot (meaning undersea boat), so the British called German submarines 'U-boats'. Inside a U-boat conditions were cramped; poor ventilation and the heat and fumes from the engine meant that the air was stuffy. U-boat crews navigated through seas full of minefields and had to avoid detection from ships above in order to attack enemy vessels.

In short supply

In 1914 one German submarine sank three British warships on the same day. Later, as the Germans began to target cargo ships, Britain was in danger of running out of food. In just one month, February 1917, German U-boats sank more than 200 ships carrying food, fuel and other supplies to Britain.

Soon, cargo ships were being fitted with guns and were sailing in convoys with warships to protect them. By 1918 German U-boats were suffering losses, too. Of 372 U-boats, 178 had been destroyed by the Allies at the end of the war.

RMS *Lusitania*

On 7 May 1915 a German submarine sank the British passenger liner RMS *Lusitania* off the coast of Ireland. The ship was bound from New York, USA, to Liverpool, England. The USA had not yet joined the war, but the attack turned many Americans against Germany.

1,198 passengers died on board RMS *Lusitania*, 128 of whom were American.

War in the Air

The First World War saw aircraft start to play a big part in war. In 1914, planes were too slow for air battles. Most were biplanes, with a top speed of about 100 miles per hour. Pilots flew over battlefields to report on enemy lines and direct artillery fire on the ground. Sometimes they shot at enemy observation balloons. These were fixed to the ground and had people in baskets peering down on battles.

The men in the observation balloons jumped to safety with parachutes – something that most aircraft pilots did not have!

Flying aces

Soon, faster planes with machine guns were fighting air battles. Fighter 'aces' became national heroes. To qualify as an ace, a pilot had to bring down ten enemy aircraft. Close combat between two fighter planes was called a 'dogfight'.

The Red Baron

Baron Manfred von Richthofen was a German pilot known as the 'Red Baron'. He was the highest-scoring ace in the war. He shot down eighty enemy aircraft in his distinctive red plane before he was killed in April 1918.

Bigger and better planes

The first bombs were dropped from the side of the aircraft by the pilot. Later, specialized bomber aircraft dropped bombs on cities, bringing air war to civilians for the first time. The war in the air became an important part of the fighting, and Britain set up the Royal Air Force (RAF), in April 1918. Until then, planes had been flown by army or navy pilots.

Germany's biggest plane was the Staaken bomber. It flew at only 80 miles per hour, but it could carry 2,000 kilograms of bombs for 500 miles.

Britain's biggest bomber was the V/1500, which was made to bomb Berlin in Germany. Only three were ready when the war ended in November 1918.

Zeppelin Raids

In the winter of 1915, the first German airships, called Zeppelins, arrived in Britain's skies. They were named after their inventor, Count Ferdinand von Zeppelin. Airships flew at up to 6,000 metres where it is very cold, and despite wearing thick clothes, the crew would often be freezing.

Zeppelins were over 150 metres long. If one flew low, people on the ground could see its huge sausage shape and hear the drone of engines. An airship's weakness was the hydrogen gas inside the balloon, which was highly explosive. If it could catch an airship, a fighter plane could try and shoot at a Zeppelin, set it on fire and bring it down.

Terror from the sky

During the First World War there were 103 air raids on Britain, fifty-one of which were by Zeppelins. They dropped bombs that killed 498 civilians and 58 soldiers and sailors. Other raids were carried out by bomber planes. By the end of the war, air raids had killed a total of 1,413 people.

Brave bomber

In June 1915, British pilot Rex Warneford brought down the German Zeppelin LZ 37. His plane did not have a machine gun, so he dropped his six bombs on the airship. He won the Victoria Cross but died when his plane crashed ten days later.

These giant Zeppelins flew over London and other towns and cities to drop bombs.

The Home Front

In Britain, families lived through the war on the Home Front. By 1916 the Army was running short of soldiers, so a law was passed to make all healthy men between eighteen and forty-one join the Army or Navy. This was called conscription. Men who refused to fight for religious or other reasons were known as conscientious objectors. There were about 16,000 of these in Britain. Many helped look after wounded soldiers or worked in factories, but about 5,000 conscientious objectors were sent to prison for disobeying the conscription laws.

People got news about the war from newspapers and magazines, newsreels at the cinema and from letters and postcards sent home by soldiers and sailors. Few people had telephones and there was no radio or television at the time.

Newsreels shown in cinemas were a popular source of war news for the people at home.

Rationing and hard times

Germany suffered worse food shortages than Britain, because the Royal Navy had cut off trade into German seaports (see page 31). To make sure everyone had enough to eat, people were asked to ration food themselves and in 1917, King George V asked British families to 'eat less bread'. Rationing was introduced in London in early 1918 and this was extended nationwide by the summer, when families were allowed to buy only limited amounts of meat, butter, margarine, sugar and jam. To make up for the shortages, people grew extra vegetables in gardens and allotments.

People in Britain saw other changes, too. Laws were passed that banned them from buying binoculars, feeding bread to horses and chickens, and setting off fireworks. New forests were planted so that the trees could provide more timber. Some rich people had their large houses turned into hospitals and lost staff as servants went off to fight on the Front or play other parts in the war effort.

Clocks were moved forward one hour, so evenings were lighter for longer and savings on lighting costs could be made. It also allowed farmers to harvest crops later in the day.

Children in the War

In the early 1900s children left school at a much younger age than they do now. In 1918, the school-leaving age was raised from twelve to fourteen. Most children above the age of thirteen would have been working; those who were at school would have learnt about the progress of the war from their teachers.

Children could not escape the sadness of war as most families had fathers, uncles or brothers fighting on the Front. In many homes there would have been photos of soldiers or sailors with a black ribbon round the photo. This showed that a loved one had died during the war.

More than 500,000 British children lost their fathers in the First World War.

Boys at the Front

The law was that no one under eighteen years of age could join the British Army, and that no one under nineteen could go to the Western Front. Thousands of boy soldiers joined up anyway and lied about their age. Older soldiers often guessed a boy was under-age if he did not shave! Some boy soldiers were found out and sent home. Others made it to the Front and some were killed.

Dick Trafford, a Lancashire coal miner, joined the army in 1914. He was just fourteen years old but pretended to be eighteen. He looked fit and strong, so there were no questions asked. Dick learned about war quickly. A new officer not sure what to do in an attack said to Dick, *'Let me follow you over [out of the trenches], and let me do what you do.'* Dick told him, *'If I happen to get hit…carry on the attack…'* The officer was killed. Though Dick was wounded and gassed in later battles, he survived and returned home at the end of the war.

Boy soldier

George Maher joined the British Army in 1916. He was thirteen when he was sent to France. Before he had even seen the trenches, George was scared. 'I was lying on my groundsheet crying in the tent when this man said, "What are you crying for?" Then it all came out, that I was only thirteen.' He was sent home and survived the war. George died in 1999.

Women at War

Women did not fight during the war. Instead, they did the jobs and work that the men fighting at the Front were not at home to do. Most would also run a household at the same time. Some women became nurses, while many others joined the Women's Army Auxiliary Corps, the Women's Royal Naval Service (both formed in 1917) or the Women's Royal Air Force.

Many poor women had always worked – in factories, on farms or as servants, but in wartime, more women did jobs in factories, hospitals, offices and shops. They also drove ambulances, buses and lorries, kept phones working and delivered letters. More than 1 million women worked in munitions factories, making explosives and guns used in the war.

Explosives are dangerous and women could be hurt or killed in accidents.

Nurses at war

Women of the Voluntary Aid
Detachment (VAD) nursed
wounded soldiers. Some nurses
went to the battlefields of
France. The crime writer
Agatha Christie was a VAD
nurse in England.

Land girls

More than 250,000
women worked on the
land. Members of the
Women's Land Army
worked on farms,
driving horse ploughs
and carts, looking
after animals and
helping with
the harvest.

Women's rights

Before the First World War women
could not vote in parliamentary or
general elections. Emmeline Pankhurst
was a suffragette, someone who
campaigned for votes for women. When
war broke out in 1914, Emmeline turned
her attention to supporting the war,
saying, 'Women are only too anxious
to be recruited'. After the war
married women over the age of thirty
were given the right to vote. This
was a major step for women's rights.

War of Words

In every country that was at war, government posters urged people to do things for their country and be patriotic. This meant supporting the war effort by fighting or doing other kinds of work for the war. One poster showed two young children asking their father: 'Daddy, what did YOU do in the Great War?' Another pictured soldiers marching away, with the words 'Women of Britain Say "GO!"'.

Propaganda

British wartime advertisements pictured cheerful soldiers at the Front drinking tea and eating biscuits. Cartoons showed German soldiers as monsters, killing women and babies. This propaganda used pictures and stories (often made up) in an attempt to show the enemy in the worst possible light. Cinema newsreels showed the battles won by the British Army, but rarely showed the battles lost.

Writers at war

Famous writers, such as Rudyard Kipling and Sir Arthur Conan Doyle, helped plan propaganda and wrote war stories. Conan Doyle brought back his famous detective Sherlock Holmes for a final adventure, an anti-German spy thriller called 'His Last Bow' (1917).

Kipling

Conan Doyle

The realities of war

Soldiers at the Front sang their own songs and wrote poetry about what war was really like. John McCrae wrote 'In Flanders Fields' in May 1915:

In Flanders fields the poppies blow
Between the crosses, row on row,
That mark our place; and in the sky
The larks, still bravely singing, fly
Scarce heard amid the guns below.

We are the Dead. Short days ago
We lived, felt dawn, saw sunset glow,
Loved and were loved, and now we lie
In Flanders fields.

Take up our quarrel with the foe:
To you from failing hands we throw
The torch; be yours to hold it high.
If ye break faith with us who die
We shall not sleep, though poppies grow
In Flanders fields.

Wilfred Owen, 1893–1918

Soldier-poet Wilfred Owen describes men after battle in his poem 'Dulce et Decorum Est':

Men marched asleep.
Many had lost their boots,
But limped on, blood-shod.
All went lame; all blind;
Drunk with fatigue.

Wilfred Owen was killed on 4 November 1918, only a week before the end of the fighting.

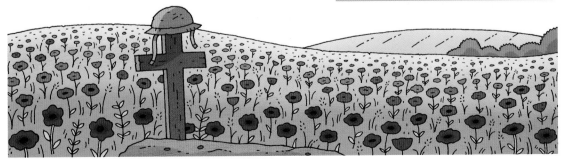

Secrets and Spies

Both sides had spies during the war. Agents reported on enemy plans and secrets. In Britain, anyone with a German-sounding name risked being called a spy. In 1917, the British royal family changed its name from the German 'Saxe-Coburg-Gotha' to the British-sounding 'Windsor'.

Code-breaking was very important during the war. Both sides sent and received messages made up of complex codes. Room 40, the Intelligence Centre at London's Admiralty, was where the German codes were broken.

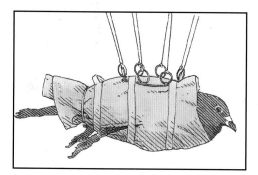

Over 500,000 homing pigeons were used to carry messages to secret agents around the world. Pigeons were even dropped by parachutes and collected by agents, before flying home with return messages.

Spying kit

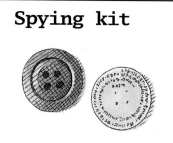

Messages could be written in the smallest of places, such as on the back of a button.

A small camera could be hidden in a pocket watch.

Invisible ink could only be read when the paper was treated by a chemical to reveal the words.

Double agent

Mata Hari was a double agent who helped both France and Germany. She was a beautiful Dutch dancer who uncovered secrets by mixing with French and German army officers. When the French found out Mata Hari was helping the Germans, too, they arrested her and she was shot as a spy in October 1917.

Secret spy

Carl Lody was a German spy in Britain. He travelled around Edinbugh, often by bicycle, spying on the British Navy. He was arrested in Ireland and shot at the Tower of London on 6 November 1914.

Brave nurse

Edith Cavell was a British nurse at a hospital in Brussels, Belgium. When Germany captured Brussels in August 1914, she hid British and French soldiers, and later helped them escape. Edith was arrested by the Germans and shot in October 1915. This caused worldwide protests and in Britain, Edith was honoured as a heroine.

America Joins the War

'Uncle Sam', a cartoon figure that represented the American people, was used on US army recruitment posters.

The United States of America remained neutral until 1917. During that year, German submarines began sinking cargo ships of any nation going to and from British ports. The targeting of American ships and the recent memory of the sinking of the RMS *Lusitania* (see page 33) turned American public opinion against Germany. When Germany suggested to Mexico that it invade the USA, it was the last straw and US President Woodrow Wilson asked Congress to declare war on Germany. It did so on 6 April 1917.

German U-boat attacks on American ships prompted the USA to join the war.

American soldiers

In early 1917, Britain and France made fresh attacks on the Western Front, but they made little progress against German defences. In June 1917, the first American troops came to Europe. US soldiers began to arrive in force in 1918, but many were inexperienced and needed to be trained.

Passchendaele

During the fighting on the Western Front, much of Ypres in Belgium had been destroyed. In the spring of 1917, the Allies planned another battle there, aiming to capture Belgian ports held by the Germans. On 7 June, near the village of Passchendaele, the British blew up nineteen mines beneath German lines on Messines Ridge. This was a success for the Allies, but the battle continued until November and is remembered as a 'muddy hell' with heavy losses on both sides.

A final push

The Germans decided to try one last attack in the spring of 1918. This included firing long-range artillery at Paris. The Germans gained ground but then the British and French, now helped by the Americans, drove back the German army, whose people at home were growing tired of war.

Tanks and planes played a big part in the final battles.

Revolution in Russia

Tsar Nicholas II

The First World War had seen nearly 2 million Russian soldiers die in battles on the Eastern Front, and by 1917 the Russian people were poor and starving. Most blamed the government of Tsar Nicholas II for their troubles.

Russia quits the war

Vladimir Lenin

By 1917 the Russian people had had enough. In March, soldiers and sailors refused to obey orders, and workers took over factories. The Tsar gave up power. The Germans, keen to get Russia out of the war, helped spark another revolution.

In April 1917 they helped the Russian Communist leader Vladimir Lenin, then in exile in Switzerland, return to Russia. He soon had to flee again, accused of being a German secret agent, but by November 1917 he was back in Russia for good. He and his followers, the Bolsheviks, took over power in Russia and made peace with Germany in March 1918.

Russia's empire crumbles

As a result of Russia's peace treaty with Germany it lost much of its old empire, including Poland, Ukraine, Estonia, Latvia and Lithuania. With Russia out of the war, Germany could now concentrate on fighting on the Western Front.

Communism

Lenin now led a Communist state – the first in the world. Communism is a political and economic system. Resources, such as mines, factories and farms are owned by the state, and wealth is shared among the people. The Communist Party ruled Russia, which then became the Soviet Union in 1922.

Reds against Whites

Russian Communists were known as 'Reds'. After the revolution, the Reds fought a bitter civil war against 'White Russians' who did not want Communism. The Allies tried to help the Whites, but were unsuccessful, and by 1922 the Red Army had won. This civil war shaped Russia's future.

Revolution in Russia was brought about by people uniting to overthrow the Tsar.

The War Ends

By the summer of 1918 all sides were exhausted and wanted peace. The last big battle on the Western Front began on 8 August 1918 and is known as the Hundred Days Offensive. The French Marshal Ferdinand Foch led the Allied armies that pushed the Germans back, and both sides more or less ended up where they had begun in 1914. Turkey signed an armistice on 31 October 1918, while in Germany, the starving people rioted and Kaiser Wilhelm II abdicated on 9 November 1918.

Ceasefire

French, British and German military leaders met in a railway carriage to sign the armistice. At 11 o'clock on the 11th day of the 11th month of 1918, for the first time in four years, the guns of war fell silent. The fighting had stopped at last.

At 5 o'clock in the morning the two sides signed the armistice agreement. It came into effect six hours later.

All over the world, people took to the streets to celebrate the end of the war.

The Treaty of Versailles

On 18 January 1919, world leaders met in Paris to work out a peace treaty that would officially end the First World War. The Treaty of Versailles was signed by the Allies and Germany on 28 June 1919. The Germans had to give up land and pay a lot of money in reparations.

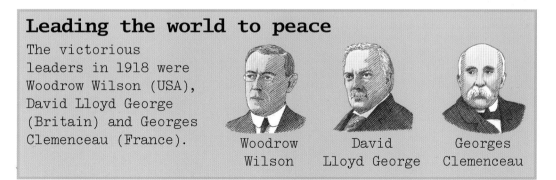

Leading the world to peace

The victorious leaders in 1918 were Woodrow Wilson (USA), David Lloyd George (Britain) and Georges Clemenceau (France).

Woodrow Wilson

David Lloyd George

Georges Clemenceau

Counting the Cost

The First World War took millions of lives. France, Belgium and Poland suffered badly because the biggest battles had been fought in these countries, destroying towns and villages. Russia and Germany lost the most soldiers.

Country	Lives lost
Germany	1.9 million
Russia	1.7 million
France	1.3 million
Austria-Hungary	1.2 million
Italy	650,000
Britain	600,000
Ottoman Empire	325,000
USA	116,000
Australia	58,150
Canada	56,500
India	43,200
New Zealand	16,130

More than 20 million soldiers were wounded, many with serious injuries that required ongoing treatment. The horrors that they saw would stay with them for the rest of their lives.

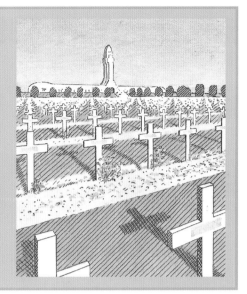

Reparations

Germany was blamed for starting the war and told to pay millions in gold every year for 35 years. It claimed its banks and businesses were so weak that it could not possibly pay that amount back. The arguments went on until, in 1933, Adolf Hitler and his Nazi party came to power. The party promised the German people that Germany would not have to repay the money and that it would get back all the land that the country had lost.

New beginnings

People hoped that life would be better after the 'war to end all wars', but the First World War left bitterness, hardship and disagreements. To try to avoid future conflicts, President Wilson of the USA proposed a League of Nations to keep the peace. It was established in 1920, but it could not prevent the Second World War which began in 1939.

Key Figures of the War

It would be impossible to mention all the people who had a significant impact on the First World War; there are far too many. Here are some of the key figures who were involved in events or who made decisions that changed the course of the war.

Georges Clemenceau (1841–1929)
Leader of the French government from 1917–1920

Marshal Ferdinand Foch (1851–1929)
French soldier, Allied Commander in Chief in 1918

Adolf Hitler (1889–1945)
A soldier in the First World War. Later led Nazi Germany into the Second World War

George V (1865–1936)
Britain's king from 1910–1936

General Douglas Haig (1861–1928)
Field Marshal who commanded the British Army on the Western Front

Horatio Herbert Kitchener, Earl Kitchener of Khartoum, (1850–1916)
British Field Marshal in charge of raising Britain's New Armies

**Paul von Hindenburg
(1847–1934)**
German Field Marshal

**Woodrow Wilson
(1856–1924)**
President of the USA
from 1913–1921

**T. E. Lawrence
(1888–1935)**
British soldier known
as 'Lawrence of Arabia'

**Vladimir Ilyich Lenin
(1870–1924)**
Leader of the Russian
Revolution in 1917

**David Lloyd George
(1863–1945)**
Welsh politician, Prime
Minister of the UK
from 1916–1922

**Kaiser Wilhelm II
(1859–1941)**
Emperor of Germany
from 1888–1918

**Tsar Nicholas II
(1868–1918)**
The last Tsar
of Russia

**Emmeline Pankhurst
(1858–1928)**
Suffragette and campaigner
for women's rights

**Marshal Joseph Joffre
(1852–1931)**
French Commander in
Chief from 1914–1916

Timeline of Main Events

1914

28 June	Austria's Archduke Franz Ferdinand is assassinated
28 July	Austria-Hungary at war with Serbia
1 August	Russia and Germany at war
3 August	Germany declares war on France
4 August	Germany invades Belgium
4 August	Britain declares war on Germany
22–30 August	Germans beat Russians at the Battle of Tannenberg
4–10 September	First Battle of Marne halts German invasion of France
29 October	Turkey joins the war
22 November	Trenches are dug along the Western Front
24–25 December	Unofficial Christmas truce

1915

22 April	First gas attack on the Western Front
25 April	Allies land at Gallipoli in Turkey
7 May	Passenger ship RMS *Lusitania* sunk by a German U-boat
23 May	Italy joins the Allies, declares war on Austria-Hungary
31 May	First Zeppelin air raids on London
12 October	Nurse Edith Cavell executed by a German firing squad
15 December	General Haig takes command of the British Army in France

1916

21 February	Germans attack French forts at Verdun
31 May–1 June	Battle of Jutland between British and German fleets
5 June	Arab Revolt against Ottoman Empire
1 July	Battle of the Somme begins in France
7 December	David Lloyd George becomes Britain's Prime Minister
18 December	Battle of Verdun ends. It is the longest battle fought on the Western Front

1917

11 March	Britain takes over Baghdad after three days of fighting
15 March	Russia's Tsar Nicholas II is forced to give up power as revolutionaries take charge in Moscow
6 April	The United States of America joins the war
7 June	The Battle of Messines Ridge
25 June	First US soldiers arrive in France
7 November	Britain captures Gaza, Palestine
10 November	Battle of Passchendaele ends
20 November	Tanks in battle at Cambrai in France
11 December	British soldiers enter Jerusalem, bringing over 600 years of Ottoman rule to an end

1918

16 January	Riots in Austria-Hungary against the war
21 March	Germany begins the Spring Offensive
1 April	Royal Flying Corps and Royal Naval Air Service combine to form the Royal Air Force (RAF)
17 July	Russia's Tsar and family are murdered
5 August	The last Zeppelin raid on Britain
30 September	British and Arab armies capture Palestine and Syria from Turkey
9 November	Kaiser Wilhelm II abdicates and flees to Holland
11 November	Germany signs the armistice agreement and fighting ends

1919

28 June	The First World War officially ends with the signing of the Treaty of Versailles

Glossary

abdicate	to formally give up power
ace	highly skilled fighter pilot who has shot down ten or more enemy aircraft
air raid	bomb attack by airship or aircraft
airship	large balloon-aircraft with engines
alliance	group of nations formally united for a cause
Allies	Britain, Russia, France and other nations united against the Central Powers
allotment	plot of land for growing food
ammunition	shells or bullets fired from guns
armistice	ceasefire agreement that stops a war
arms race	competition between two or more countries to have the most powerful armed forces
artillery	big guns able to destroy buildings and vehicles
assassinate	to murder for political purposes
battleship	large warship with big guns
bayonet	blade fixed to the end of a rifle
biplane	aircraft with two sets of wings
Bolshevik	follower of Lenin, who took power in Russia in 1917
bombard	attack with heavy artillery or bombs
British Empire	lands ruled by Britain
bunker	underground bomb shelter
cargo ship	ship that carries food or any other goods
cavalry	soldiers who fight on horseback

civilian	somebody who is not in the armed forces
code	system for disguising a message to keep it secret
colonies	an area, a country for example, that is controlled by another country or state
comrade	fellow soldier
Congress	top level of the US government
conscription	system that forces everyone (of a certain age) to join the army
convoy	group of ships or other vehicles travelling together for protection
cruiser	type of medium-sized warship
desert	to leave the army without permission
dugout	shelter built in the trenches
empire	large group of countries under the control of a single country or ruler
enlist	to sign up to the armed forces
fleet	group of warships
gas mask	breathing apparatus, worn by soldiers for protection against poison gas
gunner	army soldier who works with big guns
Home Front	term that describes the experience of the war by the people at home
Kaiser	the German or Austrian emperor
machine gun	gun that fires a lot of bullets quickly
mine	type of exploding weapon left at sea or under the ground

Glossary

munitions	weapons and explosives
newsreel	short film with news items about the war
patriotic	supporting your own country
peace treaty	agreement between countries or governments that formally ends a war
periscope	mirror device used by submarines to see above the water while still hidden below the surface
port	town or city with a harbour where ships can transfer passengers or cargo
propaganda	words and pictures that show the enemy as bad and your own side as good
reparations	payments made by Germany and her allies to Allied Nations after the war
revolt	violent refusal or objection to the authority of a government or ruler
revolution	overthrow of a government or ruler
riot	violent public disorder
RMS	Royal Mail Ship
servant	person, such as a cook or maid, who works for a better-off family
shell	container filled with explosives that is fired from a big gun
spy	person who gathers information in enemy territory
submarine	an underwater craft
tank	armoured vehicle on 'caterpillar tracks' (metal belts driven by wheels)

torpedo	weapon fired by a submarine or ship; it travels underwater to hit its target
trade	the activity of buying and selling goods and services
trenches	system of holes and tunnels to shelter soldiers from gunfire
Tsar	Russian name for emperor
ventilation	system that provides fresh air
Victoria Cross	Britain's highest award (medal) for bravery in battle
volunteer	person who offers to do something for free

Places to Visit

Imperial War Museum, London

National Army Museum, London

Firepower – The Royal Artillery Museum, London

National Maritime Museum, London

Imperial War Museum North, Manchester

National War Museum, Edinburgh

The Royal Signals Museum, Dorset

The Tank Museum, Dorset

For more information about the First World War and other resources, visit **www.ladybird.com**

Index